Seeds of a Nation

Florida

Elizabeth Weiss Vollstadt

KidHaven Press, an imprint of Gale Group, Inc.
10911 Technology Place, San Diego, CA 92127

Picture Credits
Cover Photo: © Archivo Iconografico, S.A./CORBIS
© James L. Amos/CORBIS, 23
© Archivo Iconografico, S.A./CORBIS, 8, 18, 20
© William A. Bake/CORBIS, 12
© Bettmann/CORBIS, 7, 15
© CORBIS, 33
© Historical Picture Archive/CORBIS, 6, 27
© Hulton/Archive by Getty Images, 16, 30, 35
Chris Jouan, 5, 28, 37
© The Mariners' Museum/CORBIS, 11
© North Wind Picture Archives, 25
© Joseph Sohm; Visions of America/CORBIS, 39

Library of Congress Cataloging-in-Publication Data

Vollstadt, Elizabeth Weiss, 1942–
    Florida / by Elizabeth Weiss Vollstadt.
        p. cm. — (Seeds of a Nation)
    Includes bibliographical references and index.
    Summary: Discusses Florida's early history beginning with the arrival of
Native Americans, through the era of Spanish exploration and European settlement, to secession during the Civil War.
    ISBN 0-7377-0947-2 (alk. paper)
    1. Florida—History—To 1821—Juvenile literature. 2. Florida—Histo-
ry—1821–1865—Juvenile literature. [1. Florida—History—To 1821. 2.
Florida—History—1821–1865.] I. Title. II. Series.
F314 .V85 2002
974.9—dc21

2001002965

Contents

Chapter One

Land of Many Cultures

More than one hundred years before the Pilgrims landed on Plymouth Rock, Spanish adventurers were exploring the coast of Florida. Juan Ponce de León, the first known explorer, came ashore on April 2, 1513. He named his discovery *La Florida*, the "flowery land," because its plants were so beautiful and because it was Easter time, called *Pascua Florida* (the Feast of Flowers) in Spain. But the Spaniards were not the first to come to this land. When Ponce de León arrived, he found many different Native American tribes. The story of Florida really begins with them.

Florida was first settled about ten thousand years ago by roaming hunters moving down from the north in search of food. These first Floridians were descendants of groups that came from Asia thousands of years earlier.

When the Spaniards arrived, about 350,000 native people already lived there. Among them were the

Timucuan, Apalachee, and Tocabaga tribes in the north and the Calusa, Tequesta, Ais, Jeaga, and Mayaimi tribes in the south. What we know about them comes from letters and stories left by Spanish, French, and English explorers and from **archaeologists**, scientists who study past civilizations. The most influential tribes were the Timucuans, Apalachee, and Calusa.

The Timucuans

The Timucuans were the largest group, numbering about 150,000. They lived in northeast Florida, from present-day Jacksonville west almost to the Aucilla River, about thirty miles east of Tallahassee, and south to today's Canaveral National Seashore. The

Native Tribes of Florida

Timucuans were not one tribe but different groups speaking the same language. When the Spaniards arrived, there were three main Timucuan groups, each led by a head chief who ruled over about thirty villages. Each village also had its own chief. The three groups often fought with each other.

Some Timucuan villages had only ten huts, while others had as many as fifty or sixty. These huts were round, usually about twenty feet across. They were made of small trees and grapevines, with palm fronds, or leaves, woven together to make them waterproof. The Timucuans slept on wooden benches covered with deer or bear fur. A small fire, called a smudge fire, was lit in the hut to keep bugs away, and a hole in the top allowed smoke to escape. The villages also had a large council

Timucuan villages had as many as fifty or sixty huts and a large council house for meetings.

Boys learned to fish, to hunt, and to make weapons.

house for meetings and ceremonies. Some council houses could hold as many as two thousand people.

Close relatives in the villages formed clans. Children were part of their mother's clan; their father and his relatives were in another clan. Children did not go to school. They learned the skills they needed from their clan. Girls learned how to plant corn, gather berries and fruits, prepare food, make pottery, weave baskets, and take care of children. Boys learned how to fish, hunt large animals for food and skins, and make weapons for hunting and fighting.

Timucuans were hunter-gatherers and farmers. They hunted many animals such as bears, raccoons, and deer. When they stalked deer, they disguised themselves as their prey, putting a deer's head and hide over their bodies. Along the coast, they fished and collected oysters, clams, turtles, and other seafood. Farther inland along the St. Johns River, they gathered freshwater snails. They also found blackberries, grapes, acorns, dandelion leaves, sabal palms, mushrooms, and much more. Farther west, rich soil allowed for more farming. Timucuans in this area grew corn, squash, beans, pumpkins, and sunflowers. They also grew gourds to make into bowls, and tobacco, which they smoked in ceremonies.

Apalachee Indians were skilled warriors and powerful archers.

Archaeologists know a lot about what the Timucuans ate because they tossed their waste into a big pile. Animal bones, broken pottery, and food scraps were also thrown into these trash piles. These piles grew into large mounds called **middens**. Turtle Mound, a large midden in the Canaveral National Seashore that people can visit today, is more than fifty feet high.

The Timucuans also built large burial **mounds**. They placed the body, or just the bones, on top of the ground and covered it with dirt or sand and sometimes shells. Other bodies and more sand and shells were added until the burial mound became very large. Possessions like pottery, shells, and arrowheads were placed with the remains. The more important people were, the more possessions were placed with them. Archaeologists today learn a lot about the Timucuan culture by studying these middens and mounds.

The Apalachee

The Apalachee was another important Indian group. When Ponce de León arrived, about fifty thousand Apalachee Indians lived in northwest Florida, centered around present-day Tallahassee. They were organized into tribes of five to twenty or more villages. There was a tribal chief as well as a chief in each village. The Apalachee were skilled warriors and powerful archers.

Because they lived where the soil was rich, the Apalachee grew more crops than any other Indian group. They cleared fields by cutting down trees and burning the brush. Both men and women prepared the soil, using hoes made of bone and shell. Women did the planting, and children and the elderly watched over the crops. Florida's warm climate usually allowed two growing seasons. The Apalachee grew corn, beans, squash, pumpkins, sunflowers, melons, and gourds. Like the Timucuans, they also relied on hunting, gathering, and fishing for their food.

The Calusa

Southern Florida was dominated by the Calusa Indians. Most Calusa lived in the area that is now Fort Myers and Charlotte Harbor. At home on the water, they built large canoes hollowed out of cypress-tree logs. These canoes took them into the Gulf of Mexico and also up the Caloosahatchee River to Lake Okeechobee, called Lake of Mayaimi by the Indians. The Calusa were tall, taller than the Europeans by about four inches. They were also fierce warriors who controlled other tribes and resisted the Spanish invasion.

Unlike the Timucuans, the Calusa had a strong central government. They were ruled by one main chief, called Carlos by the Spaniards. Carlos's power was so great that some explorers called him *el Rey*, meaning "the king." As a sign of respect, lesser chiefs and even chiefs from smaller tribes brought him gifts of feathers, hides, mats, food, and captives.

The Calusa did little farming, relying mostly on the sea for food. They fished by using nets made from the

Calusa Indians carved canoes out of cypress-tree logs.

fibers of cabbage palms, and they gathered shellfish such as clams and oysters. They also hunted deer and other animals and ate berries, fruits, and roots. Because of the heat, they wore little clothing. The men wore coverings, similar to shorts, made of deerskin and fastened with fancy belts that showed their position in the tribe. Women wore clothing of woven Spanish moss and palmetto leaves.

The Calusa built their villages on mounds made of earth and shells, and then surrounded them with deep moats, or ditches, for protection. Their capital and largest city was Calos, now known as Mound Key,

Large mounds like the ones seen here served as the foundations for Calusa villages.

located near the mouth of the Caloosahatchee River. Mound Key is a circular island, about 125 acres, with a canal cutting across it. The Calusa built large mounds of earth and shells to serve as foundations for their huts, temples, and other important buildings. Large middens also cover parts of the island.

The Florida Indians fought to protect their land and preserve their way of life, but they were no match for the powerful Europeans who would soon come searching for wealth and glory.

Chapter Two

Spanish Explorers Seek Wealth and Glory

Some legends say that Ponce de León was searching for the Fountain of Youth when he discovered Florida. However, he was more likely looking for gold and the glory of conquest, for himself and for the king of Spain.

On his first visit, Ponce de León landed at what is now Melbourne, just south of Cape Canaveral. He sailed south to Biscayne Bay in Miami, around the Florida Keys, and up to Charlotte Harbor, near present-day Fort Myers. He met Timucuan and Calusa Indians, and in both cases he and his men were attacked.

After several clashes with the Calusa, Ponce de León returned to Puerto Rico, but he came back to Florida in 1521 to establish a colony on the southwest coast. Once again, the fierce Calusa Indians attacked. This time Ponce de León was wounded in the thigh by an arrow. He and his men left Florida and traveled to Cuba, where Ponce de León died of his wound.

Narváez Searches for Gold

Other explorers, called **conquistadores**, soon followed. Pánfilo de Narváez hoped to find in Florida the gold and wealth that the Spanish explorer Hernán Cortés had found in Mexico. Narváez arrived at Tampa Bay in 1528 and selected about three hundred of his four hundred men to go ashore with him. He sent the remaining men—and all of their supplies—farther north to find another harbor and wait for the explorers.

Marching into Florida, Narváez used force and cruelty in dealing with the Indians. One story says that he chopped off the nose of a chief when the chief would not tell him where some gold ornaments came from. Finally, the Indians told Narváez that he could find gold in the north, where the Apalachee Indians lived. Narváez and his men headed north to find it.

But the gold-laden cities remained a dream. Instead of riches, they found hunger, heat, and dense tropical forests. Adding to their troubles, they angered the native people by treating them badly. In Apalachee territory, for example, they came upon a main Indian village, took the

Legends say Ponce de León was searching for the Fountain of Youth when he discovered Florida.

chief hostage, and seized the corn that the Indians had stored.

The Apalachee fought back, using their skills in archery. Álvar Núñez Cabeza de Vaca, a member of the Spanish **expedition**, later wrote, "Tall and naked, at a distance [the Apalachee] appear giants. . . . Their bows are as thick as an arm, seven feet long, shooting an arrow at 200 paces with unerring [perfect] aim."[1]

Many of Narváez's men became sick, and their food supplies ran low. Finally, they gave up their quest for gold. Forty men had died of hunger or sickness, and twelve had been killed by Indians. They hoped to find the ships that they had sent north, but the two groups never found each other. The nearly 250 people who were

Cabeza de Vaca and three other men were the only survivors from Pánfilo de Narváez's expedition.

left built rafts and tried to sail to Spanish settlements in Mexico. They did not succeed. Some men drowned, including Narváez. Others were washed ashore. In the end, only four men survived to reach Mexico City in June 1536.

De Soto Takes Up the Quest

Despite the failure of the Narváez expedition, Spanish explorers were not discouraged. They still believed that gold could be found in Florida. One conquistador, Hernando de Soto, had marched with Francisco Pizarro when he conquered the Inca empire in South

America. De Soto's share of that expedition made him wealthy and eager for more.

In 1539, de Soto landed at Tampa Bay with about seven hundred men and two women. They unloaded vicious dogs trained to attack, 220 horses, and supplies, including a herd of pigs to drive along and eat as needed. Shortly after landing, they met Juan Ortiz, a survivor of the Narváez expedition who had been captured by Indians. Ortiz became a guide and interpreter.

De Soto in Apalachee Territory

Like Narváez, de Soto headed north to the Apalachee territory, hoping to find gold. De Soto treated the Indians as cruelly as Narváez had. He wrecked villages and took their food. He captured hundreds of villagers to act as guides and to carry supplies. Some were chained together. He also took chiefs as hostages, killed those who resisted his army, and sometimes cut off their hands or noses as an example of what would happen to those who tried to stop his march.

Some natives fought back with bows and arrows. Others burned their huts and crops and retreated. Native guides who had been captured often led de Soto away from villages and into traps where Indians were hiding and waiting to attack.

De Soto spent his first winter in Anhaica, the main village of the Apalachee, part of present-day Tallahassee. Still seeking riches, he left Florida and spent the next three years marching through other parts of North America.

In addition to destroying villages, de Soto and his men left behind a trail of diseases, such as smallpox, measles, and typhoid fever, that had not existed in the New World. Thousands of natives died from these diseases. De Soto himself died in May 1542 of an unknown disease. More than a year later, 311 survivors of his expedition reached a Spanish settlement in Mexico.

In defense of their families and villages, some natives fought de Soto with bows and arrows.

Spanish explorers never found the gold they were seeking in Florida. Nor did they establish any settlements. After two more attempts to found a colony, King Philip II announced in 1561 that Spain would not send any more expeditions to Florida. However, he would soon change his mind.

The French Settle on the St. Johns River

Although Spain claimed all of North America for itself, France believed that lands that had not been settled were open to anyone. An early French expedition in 1562, led by Jean Ribault, failed, and Ribault returned to Europe. But two years later, a second expedition of three hundred men and four women established Fort Caroline on a small bluff near the mouth of the river May, today's St. Johns River. The fort was triangle shaped and contained palm-covered huts built with help from the Timucuans, who were friendly and eager to trade. One of the colonists was artist Jacques Le Moyne, whose pictures still appear in books today. They provide insights into life in Indian and colonial Florida.

Many of the colonists in Fort Caroline were Huguenots, French Protestants looking for religious freedom. However, most of the people who settled there were seeking adventure and riches. The colony was located near Spanish shipping lanes, and the colonists were more interested in plundering treasure-laden ships heading home to Spain than they were in

King Philip II ended Spanish expeditions to Florida after his explorers failed to find gold.

farming. By the time Ribault returned to the New World with six hundred more settlers, the colony was failing. Ribault knew the Spanish had learned about Fort Caroline and prepared for an attack.

Ribault was right to fear the Spanish. They did not want the French in North America and were angry that French settlers were stealing the goods from their ships.

The Spanish king sent Pedro Menéndez de Avilés, an experienced naval officer, to destroy Fort Caroline.

Spain Establishes St. Augustine

Menéndez arrived in Florida on August 28, 1565. Because it was the day dedicated to St. Augustine on the Catholic Church's calendar, he named his colony St. Augustine. With him were five hundred soldiers, two hundred sailors, and one hundred civilians. Meanwhile, at Fort Caroline, Ribault decided to attack first, and he sailed for St. Augustine with his men. But the weather turned against him. A tropical storm scattered his ships and stranded the survivors on present-day Daytona Beach and Cape Canaveral. Menéndez was able to march overland to Fort Caroline and easily take control of the colony.

After returning to St. Augustine, Menéndez and his forces found and killed the French soldiers who had survived the storm. (Today, the inlet where this occurred is called Matanzas, which means "slaughter.") The French flag was gone. Florida was safely in Spanish hands and would remain so for the next two hundred years.

Chapter Three

New Flags over Florida

Spain knew that it had to have settlements in Florida in order to keep control in North America. In the spring of 1569, almost three hundred settlers arrived in St. Augustine from farming areas in Spain. Some were sent to St. Elena in what is now South Carolina; others remained in St. Augustine. The settlers at St. Augustine built wooden houses with roofs made of palm leaves. They planted orange trees and learned how to grow corn, which soon replaced wheat as one of the most important parts of their diet. Cattle grazed on common land.

The St. Augustine colonists had several types of jobs. Some were craftsmen or tradesmen—peddlers, shoemakers, moneylenders, tavern keepers, fishermen, hunters, blacksmiths, and carpenters. Some of the soldiers' wives ran boardinghouses. Other colonists harvested trees such as juniper and oak and exported the wood. Still others began trading fur with the Indians and producing tar and pitch. (Tar and pitch are substances made from trees that are used for waterproofing, sealing, and paving.)

St. Augustine became the center of Spanish activity in North America, but it was often attacked and plundered by pirates. In 1672, construction began on a large fort to protect the settlement. Called the Castillo de San Marcos (Castle of St. Mark), the fort was completed in 1695.

The thick walls of the fort were built of **coquina**, a type of limestone made up of tiny mollusk shells cemented together. When hit by a cannonball, the walls of the fort did not shatter. Instead, they were dented by

The Castillo de San Marcos still stands today and is popular with tourists.

the ball but remained intact. Historian Michael Gannon wrote that, after two attacks, the fort "looked like a chocolate chip cookie."[2] The fort was so strong that it never fell to enemy attack. Today, the Castillo de San Marcos is a national monument visited by thousands of tourists each year.

The Florida Missions

The Spanish wanted to settle in Florida for another reason as well. They believed they had a duty to convert the Indians to Catholicism. The efforts to establish **missions** also supported Spain's political goals. The Spanish hoped that once the native population became Christian, they would become loyal to Spain and would help protect Florida from invaders.

Missionary work existed throughout Spanish exploration, but the real work of converting the Indians began when the Franciscan priests arrived in 1573. Most of the priests were truly religious men dedicated to helping the Indians. They worked hard, enduring hunger, tribal warfare, long journeys through dense forests, unbearable heat, and mosquitoes.

Within sixty years, the Franciscan missions successfully spread out across the northern third of Florida, where the Timucuan and Apalachee Indians lived. These tribes had stable villages and were used to farming, making it easier for them to accept European ideas of work. Attempts to Christianize the Calusa and other southern tribes failed.

A priest teaches an Indian about Christianity.

Indians were taught the Roman Catholic catechism, or the religion's beliefs. They also learned new skills such as carpentry, weaving, and caring for domestic animals. Some Indians were taught to read and write Spanish. One priest, Francisco Pareja, taught the Timucuans how to read and write in their own language.

The priests tried to get rid of Indian traditions. They insisted that Indians take Spanish names at baptism and that the men cut their long hair. They banned dances related to Indian religious customs and no longer allowed men to have more than one wife. Once the Indians were baptized, they became Spanish subjects and had to obey Spanish law. They were often required to work for the Spaniards for little or no pay. The Indians would agree for a while, but sometimes the pull of their old ways was too strong. Many also resented some priests' increasing demands that they do more and more work without payment. Rebellions were not uncommon.

During this time, too, the Indian population continued to decline as a result of deaths from European diseases. From 1649 to 1656, a series of epidemics, or diseases that affected a large number of people in one area, swept through Timucuan villages. In 1659, another epidemic killed ten thousand Apalachee.

In the end, however, the missions were destroyed by the rivalry between Spain and England. In 1702, English soldiers and Creek Indians, led by Governor James Moore of Carolina, attacked St. Augustine and the missions. They never took St. Augustine and the Castillo de San Marcos, but later raids of the Indian missions did succeed. The invaders were sometimes helped by the mission Indians themselves. Those who stayed loyal to the missions and refused to surrender to the English and Creek were captured and taken to Carolina as slaves.

The End of the First Spanish Period

Unfortunately for Spain, Florida never attracted enough Spanish families to become a successful colony. And ties with the Indians were not strong enough to produce strong allies. In the 1750s, two hundred years after its founding, St. Augustine was still a small town filled with soldiers and a few settlers. On the west coast, Pensacola was a fort and a few houses.

Then, in 1761, Spain made the mistake of siding with France in the French and Indian War (1754–1763), which was fought over control of North America. Britain immediately took over the rich Spanish port of Havana, Cuba. When Britain won the war in 1763, Spain had to give Florida to England in order to regain Havana. Most Spanish citizens fled to Havana. A new era began in Florida.

Spanish citizens retreated to Cuba after the French and Indian War.

Twenty Years of British Rule

The British flag now flew over St. Augustine and other settlements in Florida. Because of Florida's size, Britain divided it into two colonies, East and West. East Florida, with its capital at St. Augustine, stretched from the Atlantic Ocean to the Apalachicola River (about forty-five miles west of present-day Tallahassee). West Florida, with Pensacola as its capital, extended all the way to the Mississippi River, including parts of present-day Alabama, Louisiana, and Mississippi. As with the Spanish missions, the settlement was mainly across the northern third of the state.

The British actively encouraged immigration and were more successful than the Spanish in bringing

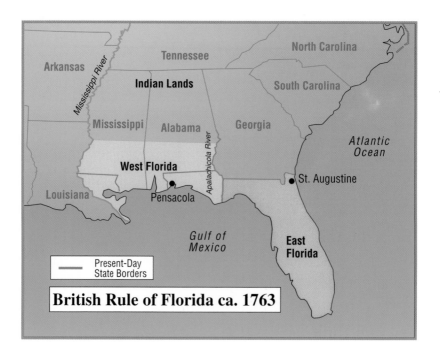

British Rule of Florida ca. 1763

families to their new colonies. Pioneers were given land to farm. Slavery was allowed to make Florida attractive to settlers from Britain's southern colonies. Farmers from Alabama and West Georgia settled in West Florida. East Florida attracted Europeans and southern planters who established large rice and indigo plantations. Blacks, most of them slaves, made up most of the population.

The Creek

The Creek Indian tribes also moved into Florida and replaced the original tribes, whose numbers continued to decline. Some of the Creek had participated in the raids on the Apalachee missions and had remained there ever since. Others came later as white colonists in Georgia moved onto their land. The English eventually called them Seminole, taken from the Spanish word *cimmarones*, which means "wild ones" or "runaways."

Florida and the American Revolution

Both East and West Florida remained loyal to Britain during the American Revolution. Their colonists were new and depended on Britain. Thousands of Tory refugees (those who supported Britain) fled to Florida from the thirteen rebellious colonies. The Castillo de San Marcos, now called Fort St. Mark, became a prison. Three signers of the Declaration of Independence—Arthur Middleton, Thomas Heyward Jr., and Edward Rutledge—were imprisoned there.

A young Creek Indian.

In 1783, however, Florida was returned to Spain by the Treaty of Paris, signed after the Americans won their war of independence. The Spanish flag would fly once more.

The Second Spanish Period

Many English settlers left Florida when Spain regained control, but they were not replaced by Spanish immigrants. Instead, new settlers came from England and the new United States. These Anglo-Americans soon began calling for independence. In 1810, a group of settlers around present-day Baton Rouge, Louisiana, established their own government. Then, in 1813, the United States took over the western part of West Florida, up to what is now the western boundary of the state.

In East Florida, too, areas such as Amelia Island in the north declared independence. During the War of 1812, which involved the United States and Britain, British forces seized the fort at Pensacola and encouraged Creek Indian raids against the Americans. When the Creek destroyed Fort Mims in Alabama, American general Andrew Jackson invaded Florida to chase after the Creek and force the British from Pensacola. He returned in 1818 to fight the Seminole Indians in what is now called the First Seminole War. He continued south, finally demanding the surrender of Spanish forts in Pensacola.

Realizing that it had lost control of Florida, Spain turned over the territory to the United States in 1819. In the summer of 1821, Andrew Jackson returned to Florida as its first military governor. An exchange of flags took place at ceremonies in St. Augustine and Pensacola. Florida was now a U. S. possession, and for the first time, the American flag flew over its towns.

Chapter Four

From Territory to State

Florida officially became a territory of the United States on March 4, 1822. Congress organized East and West Florida into a single territory and named William Duval the first civil governor. Working with Duval was a secretary and a legislature called the Legislative Council. All were appointed by the president. To be fair to both the east and west areas of Florida, the council was supposed to hold half of its meetings in St. Augustine and half in Pensacola. However, traveling between the cities was long and dangerous. One ship carrying council representatives from St. Augustine to Pensacola ran into storms and arrived six weeks late. A more central site was needed, one that was located midway between the two. Tallahassee, where the Apalachee had once ruled, was selected to be the territory's capital.

Slaves work on a Florida cotton field, one of many established by wealthy plantation owners.

This middle Florida area, between the Apalachicola and Suwannee Rivers, began to attract the majority of settlers, many of them from wealthy southern families who came to establish sugar and cotton plantations in the fertile soil. Dependent on slave labor, this middle region had much in common with the American South. Soon it became the dominant area of Florida, with the wealthy plantation owners holding much political power. The region's population grew, too, from twenty-four hundred in 1825 to thirty-four thousand in 1840. By contrast, in 1835, western Florida had only fifty-five hundred people and eastern Florida, fifteen thousand.

To support this growth, Florida needed transportation systems. Roads were built connecting St. Augustine to Pensacola, Jacksonville to New Smyrna, and Tampa Bay to the Suwannee River. Four short railway lines were also built.

More land was also needed for settlement. When the United States took over Florida, it agreed to honor valid Spanish titles to land in the territory. Some cases involving Spanish and English claims to land dragged through the courts for years. Finally, commissions were set up to examine disagreements over land. Gradually, they were settled, and more land became available to American settlers.

The Seminole Wars

The increase in white settlers created conflicts with the Seminole Indians, because the Americans wanted the land the Indians occupied in the northern part of the territory. White settlers complained that the Seminole stole their cattle and provided protection to their runaway slaves. Governor Duval demanded that the five thousand Seminole living near Tallahassee move somewhere else, but they refused. Angry white settlers wrote letters to the governor and to the president.

In 1823, the Seminole were pressured into signing the Treaty of Moultrie Creek, which gave them a reservation of 4 million acres in the southern interior of Florida, north of the Fort Myers area but south of Ocala. Peace did not last long. Unhappy with the reservation, some Seminole returned to their homes in the north and the white settlers continued to push for the Seminole's total removal from the state. In 1828, the Florida Legislative Council urged Congress to remove all the Seminole Indians from Florida. The council had support from Andrew Jackson, the president of the United States, who believed that all Indian tribes should be moved west of the Mississippi.

In 1833, again under pressure, Indian chiefs signed the Treaty of Fort Gibson, agreeing to move to areas of present-day Arkansas and Oklahoma. Many Indians

Seminole warrior Osceola (pictured) and his tribe were pushed out of Florida by white settlers.

rebelled at this agreement, however. Under the leadership of a young warrior named Osceola, they launched the Second Seminole War, which lasted from 1835 to 1842. During the war, Osceola was betrayed and captured under a flag of truce. He died in prison in 1838. Like the original Florida natives, the Seminole were no match for the white man's power. Those who were not killed were shipped west. By April 1842, only about three or four hundred Indians remained in Florida. They were allowed to stay on a reservation in the south that included Lake Okeechobee and the Everglades.

But farmers and cattlemen decided that they wanted even that piece of land since the soil was so rich around the lake. Again, the Seminole resisted, resulting in the Third Seminole War. By 1858, the small number of Indians left were forced to withdraw into the Everglades. There, they survived and succeeded in keeping their traditions and culture. They continue to be a force in Florida today.

Becoming a State

During the Seminole wars, some Floridians began to push for making Florida a state. But not all agreed. The wealthy plantation owners, who already had much political power, supported statehood. But small farmers, cattlemen, and northern investors in the east were afraid that becoming a state would mean higher taxes and more power for the plantation owners. They wanted statehood to wait.

FLORIDA'S PLACE IN THE UNITED STATES TODAY

In addition, the two groups had many disagreements. Bank policies, for example, favored large landowners over small farmers, and small farmers wanted more access to loans. Another issue was the makeup of the state itself. Eastern Florida wanted the territory to become two states, the middle wanted one state, and western Florida discussed becoming part of Alabama.

Despite conflicts, the movement to become a state pushed on. Richard Call, Florida's third governor, called a constitutional convention in December 1838. After they agreed on changes to the bank policy and state loans, the representatives approved a constitution in January 1839. The people narrowly approved it later that year by a vote of 2,070 to 1,953. Still, it took six more years for Florida to be accepted as a state. Some people argued that the population and taxable wealth could not support a state government. Other obstacles were the Seminole wars, bank failures throughout the country in 1837, and poor cotton crops in 1840 and 1841.

However, David Levy Yulee, Florida's territorial representative to Congress from 1841 to 1845, continued to press for statehood. In Florida, he wrote letters, gave lectures, and published pamphlets. He created a consensus in support of one state rather than two and persuaded Florida voters that statehood was the road to increased wealth and importance. In January 1845, the House of Representatives approved the admission of Florida into the United States. On March 3, Florida became the twenty-seventh state.

Florida's Continued Growth

Less than twenty years later, during the American Civil War, Florida joined the southern states in seceding, or separating, from the United States. Yet another flag, the Confederate, flew over the state. Once the Civil War was over, however, and Florida rejoined the United States,

The Florida flag, a symbol of the twenty-seventh state to join the United States.

Florida entered an era of tremendous growth that has continued until today. From slightly more than 2 million people in 1940, Florida's population grew to nearly 5 million in 1960, more than 9 million in 1980, and almost 16 million in 2000. Tourism is a major industry and many more visitors flood into the state each winter to enjoy the mild climate.

Much of Florida is now developed, but visitors to national seashores and state parks can still feel the beauty of Ponce de León's *La Florida*. And in the old city of St. Augustine, they can still hear the echoes of Spanish footsteps.

Facts About Florida

State capital: Tallahassee

Largest city: Jacksonville (735,617 people)

State nickname: The Sunshine State

State motto: In God We Trust (unofficial)

State song: "Old Folks at Home," also called "Suwannee River"

State tree: Sabal palm

State bird: Mockingbird

State flower: Orange blossom

Resident population (2000 estimate): 15,982,378

Ethnic mix: White, 78%; Hispanic or Latino, 16.8%; African American, 14.6%; Asian, 1.7%; American Indian/Alaskan native, 0.3%; Hawaiian or other Pacific Islander native, 0.1% (Hispanics may also be included under other races, which is why the total is greater than 100%)

Natural resources: Sandy beaches, sunny climate, thick forests, and minerals (limestone, phosphate, peat, sand, gravel, clay, and mineral sands such as ilmenite, rutile, and zircon)

Trees: Ash, beech, bald cypress, hickory, magnolia, mangrove, maple, oak, pine, sweet gum, and various types of palm trees

Flowers: Iris, lily, lupine, orchid, sunflower, climbing vines such as jasmine and morning glory, azalea, camellia, gardenia, hibiscus, oleander, poinsettia, and bougainvillea

Animals: Black bear, deer, gray fox, panther, wildcat, opossum, otter, raccoon, squirrel, turtle, and alligator

Birds: In addition to common eastern birds such as the cardinal, mockingbird, blue jay, and whippoorwill, Florida has the largest colonies of pelicans, egrets, herons, anhinga, and ibises north of the Caribbean.

Marine Life: Shrimp, lobster, grouper, clams, mackerel, mullet, swordfish, tuna, menhaden, oysters, scallops, sharks, bass, and catfish

Important crops: Oranges and other citrus fruits, tomatoes, sugar cane, greenhouse and nursery products, peanuts, soybeans, tobacco, and vegetables such as cabbage, celery, cucumbers, green peppers, lettuce, potatoes, snap bean, squashes, and sweet corn

Notes

Chapter 2: Spanish Explorers Seek Wealth and Glory

1. Quoted in Michael Gannon, ed., *The New History of Florida*. Gainesville: University Press of Florida, 1996, p. 23.

Chapter 3: New Flags over Florida

2. Michael Gannon, *Florida: A Short History*. Gainesville: University Press of Florida, 1993, p. 15.

Glossary

archaeologist: A scientist who learns about past civilizations by studying the physical things they left behind, such as pottery, tools, and graves.

conquistador: Someone who conquers another people, usually used to refer to the Spanish soldiers who defeated and plundered the civilizations of the New World.

coquina: A building material of a soft, porous limestone made up of fragments of coral and the shells of mollusks, such as oysters, snails, and clams.

expedition: A journey to explore new lands. The group of people who take such a journey is also called an expedition.

midden: A trash pile. Middens left by native tribes in Florida consisted mostly of shells from sea animals such as snails, oysters, and clams, as well as other animal bones and pieces of pottery.

mission: A place established by religious people to teach others about their faith. Missions consisted of a church, a school, a hut for the priest, and often a hut for Indians who lived and worked at the mission.

mound: A large pile of earth or stones that served as a burial place. Some Florida Indians also built temple mounds for their religious ceremonies.

For Further Exploration

Books

Hal Bamford, *Florida History*. 2nd ed. St. Petersburg, FL: Great Outdoors, 1976. This book briefly covers the history of the state from the early Indians through 1976. Each chapter ends with a summary and a series of study questions, as well as suggested projects to learn more about the period of history discussed.

Suzanne M. Coil, *Florida*. New York: Franklin Watts, 1987. *Florida* gives a brief history of the state, plus information about modern Florida. It covers topics such as people, economy, tourism, wildlife, conservation, climate, education, and government.

Florida: Fun and Facts. Forest City, FL: T.N.T. Creations, 1983. This short book has pictures and facts about Florida, including its Indians, history, wildlife, plant life, seashore, and lighthouses.

J. Carver Harris, *Castillo: The Dramatic Story of Spain's Great 17th Century Fortress in St. Augustine*. Jacksonville, FL: J. Carver Harris, 1982. The history of Castillo de San Marcos is told using text and large black-and-white photographs.

Virginia Driving Hawk Sneve, *The Seminoles*. New York: Holiday House, 1994. Colorful drawings illustrate this beautiful book which presents the history of the Seminole Indians from their Creek ancestors, through the Seminole wars, and up to present day.

Kelley G. Weitzel, *The Timucua Indians: A Native American Detective Story*. Gainesville: University Press of Florida, 2000. This easy-to-read book tells about these early people—where and how they lived, what they ate, what their families were like, and what games they played. It is an interactive book with line drawings, where readers are encouraged to discover information themselves and come to conclusions about the Timucuans and about the study of history.

Websites

M. C. Bob Leonard, *The Floridians: A Social History of Florida*. www.floridahistory.org/floridians/textpg.htm.

This website has many sections, each telling about a different part of Florida's history and each with many links for more information.

"Timucua Kids Page," *Florida Indians*.http://pelotes.jea.com/ kidtimuc.htm#Timucuan%20Kid%20Page

This site answers ten basic questions about the Timucuan Indians. There are also links to more information about Florida Indians written in a more adult style.

Index